A MOTHER'S LITTLE
INSTRUCTION BOOK

Mummy

A MOTHER'S LITTLE INSTRUCTION BOOK

JASMINE BIRTLES

BOXTREE

First published in Great Britain in 1997 by
Boxtree Limited
an imprint of Macmillan Books, 25 Eccleston Place, London SW1W 9NF

10 9 8 7 6 5 4 3 2

ISBN: 0 7522 1104 8

Cover design: Shoot That Tiger!
Page design: Nigel Davies

Printed and bound in the United Kingdom by Redwood Books, Trowbridge,
Wiltshire.
A CIP catalogue entry for this book is available from the British Library.

Some mothers do 'ave 'em, and you've got this book. Lucky you! Mothering is the hardest job in the world and there's no time off for good behaviour – even with OXO cubes. In Africa mothers return to the fields within hours of giving birth. And the way the NHS is going, well … Of course, motherhood does have its joys – but that's another book. So, stick the kids in front of the telly, banish their dad to the garden, lock yourself in the loo and have a giggle over this book.

MUMMY

You know you've lost control of your children when you're the one that gets locked in your room.

• • •

If the children are really naughty use a high-security playpen. Once they've settled down you can climb out.

Mummy

Great car games to play with the children:
'Sleeping Dragons' – everyone whispers
so they don't wake the dragons;
'Trappist Monks' – everyone
communicates by sign language only;
'Church Mouse' – everyone stays
completely silent for the entire journey.

7

Mummy

A new Olympic event:
Doing the weekly shop with children
and dog in tow.

• • •

Postnatal depression shouldn't
last more than eighteen years.

mummy

8

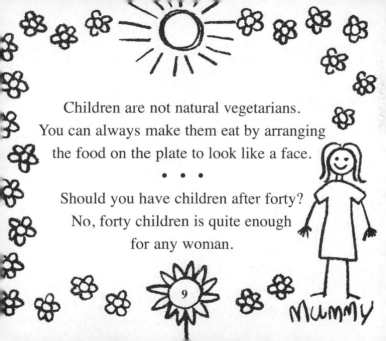

Children are not natural vegetarians.
You can always make them eat by arranging
the food on the plate to look like a face.

• • •

Should you have children after forty?
No, forty children is quite enough
for any woman.

9

You know you've been a successful mother
if your children grow up earning enough to
pay for their own counselling.

• • •

If you really want your child to do
something, forbid them to do it.

Mummy

You're a mother if you constantly watch your children for signs of improvement – even when they're middle-aged.

• • •

A mother is someone who dreams of going back to work for a rest.

11

mummy

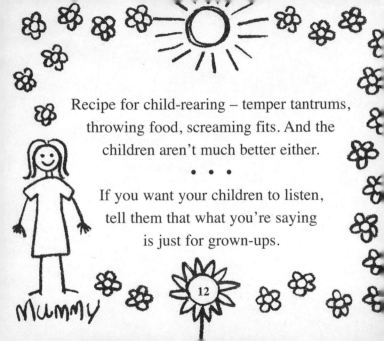

Recipe for child-rearing – temper tantrums,
throwing food, screaming fits. And the
children aren't much better either.

• • •

If you want your children to listen,
tell them that what you're saying
is just for grown-ups.

Mummy

12

Children are like waiters – they never
come when you call them and they take
no notice of your orders.

• • •

The amazing thing about babies is that
they're constantly progressing –
from one nappy to another.

13

Mummy

There is no such thing as an
unemployed mother.

• • •

School days are the best days
of your life – except for the washing,
ironing, darning…

Mummy

14

Anyone who says that nature is wonderful
has never had to change a nappy.

• • •

Only have one child. That way you will
have more time to yourself and you'll
always know who did it.

Mummy

Having a baby in a private hospital means paying for something for which you did all the work.

• • •

Women with babies and women without babies always feel envious of each other.

16

Mummy

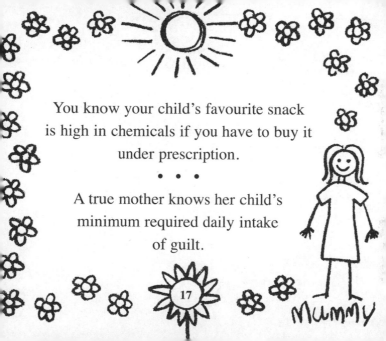

You know your child's favourite snack is high in chemicals if you have to buy it under prescription.

• • •

A true mother knows her child's minimum required daily intake of guilt.

17

mummy

Mothers have a sixth sense
about their children –
they always know if someone's
trying to flush a cat
down the toilet.

18

Mummy

Mothers of small children worry about E numbers. Mothers of teenagers worry about the numbers of E.

• • •

Kids grow out of clothes so fast you should buy them on a timeshare basis.

19

Mummy

If the hand that rocks the cradle rules the world how come it's not even paid a minimum wage?

• • •

The division of duties between parents usually means that one wears the trousers and the other wears the sick.

20

Mothering is the best all-round job.
No other career would allow you
to be plumber, drill sergeant, nurse,
chef, umpire, banker, telephonist
and international diplomat –
all before 9.30 a.m.

Mum's pressies:
What she wants
– A romantic weekend for two in Paris
– A Valentino evening dress
– A total pamper day at a health farm

Mummy

22

What she gets
– A family bucket of KFC nuggets
– A wipe-clean apron with
'Mum's The Best' written on it
– Lavender bath salts from Superdrug

23

Mummy

Motherhood: a 20-year, non-refundable
ticket to a domestic ghetto.

• • •

Don't bother taking your children
to the zoo. If the zoo wants them
it'll come and get them.

24

Mummy

Telling a child to have a pee before a long car journey never works. The only thing that will make him want to go is a sign saying 'No services for 50 miles'.

25

Mummy

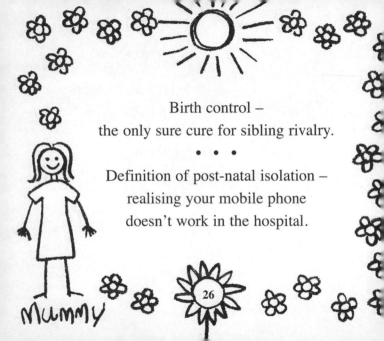

Birth control –
the only sure cure for sibling rivalry.

• • •

Definition of post-natal isolation –
realising your mobile phone
doesn't work in the hospital.

Mummy

26

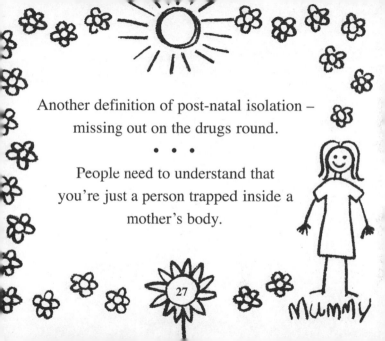

Another definition of post-natal isolation –
missing out on the drugs round.

• • •

People need to understand that
you're just a person trapped inside a
mother's body.

27

Mummy

There is never a right time to have a baby,
but the middle of a top-level board-meeting
is probably about as wrong as it gets.

• • •

Babies' luggage makes Ivana Trump
look frugal.

Mummy

28

Taking a small child to the shops
needs as much preparation as a
mountaineering expedition.
At 18 the same child will set off
for a round-the-world trip with
a rucksack the size of a filofax.

Mummy

A supermarket trolley can contain a child – but only if you put him under the groceries.

• • •

If you buy a second-hand pram, check its MOT. Has it been used by a Mother Of Twins?

Three things are needed when feeding a baby – patience, love and a wetsuit.

• • •

Mothering is learned through experience and word of mouth. This year's word is 'Prozac'.

31

If you have a two-storey house
have two sets of nappy-changing kits –
one upstairs and one downstairs.
Two sets of husbands
would be handy too.

Mummy

32

Check out local outlets for
second-hand baby equipment –
but remember that you'll be
disappointed if you're hoping
to find second-hand babies.

33

Mummy

Why do friends and relatives always give your children toys for Christmas when all you really want is MONEY?

• • •

This year's colour for mums is beige. Actually it's any year's colour for mums.

34

mummy

Babies are great at billiards
and being bilious. Even the most
uncoordinated infant can
rival Steve Davis when it comes
to potting the green.

35

mummy

The problem with children is they refuse
to behave the way you think you did
when you were a girl.

• • •

A silent child is a contented child –
and a mother with earplugs.

Mummy

36

Motherly love is a binding contract,
but you can add the small print yourself.

• • •

Motherhood demands liberal quantities
of discipline… sorry, gin.

Mummy

Fathers used to be shut out
of the birth. These days you can
hear the door slamming
right after the conception.

• • •

Recipe for disaster –
a hungry child in a clean kitchen.

Mummy

38

When your child gets difficult
take her out for a walk. If she's
really difficult take her out for a run...
with Linford Christie.

• • •

Children only cry when mum
sees them fall over.

39

Mummy

Children lose everything
they play with so give them
your husband's hat –
the one that should have been
thrown away a decade ago.

Mummy

40

To save time on busy mornings
buy your children shoes
with velcro fastenings.
To save even more time velcro
their feet to a skateboard.

41

Mummy

The words 'holds 12 pounds'
on the side of a pack
of nappies refers to the weight
of the baby, not how much
poo it can take.

42

Mummy

Proven scientific fact:
rings of Saturn are made up
of those essential
lost parts of your
child's toys.

43

Mummy

Bringing up your first child is like
playing a saxophone in public and learning
the instrument as you go along.

· · ·

You know your toddler is hungry
when he starts to
eat his own pasta collage.

44

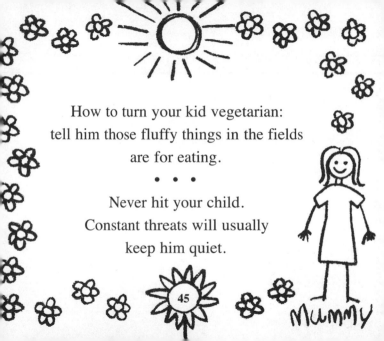

How to turn your kid vegetarian:
tell him those fluffy things in the fields
are for eating.

• • •

Never hit your child.
Constant threats will usually
keep him quiet.

45

Mummy

If you've wondered why
your teenager gets lost in thought it's
because it's unfamiliar territory.

• • •

'Son' is a good word for a little boy
because each one believes the world
revolves around him.

Mothers have no excuse
not to love their children – at least they
know they're their own.

• • •

There's nothing wrong
with teenage girls that reasoning
won't aggravate.

Mummy

A woman who miscalculates
is called a mother.

• • •

A mother always knows where
things are. That's why the rest of
the family resent them so much.

MUMMY

48

It takes a mother 18 years to make her son into a man and a girlfriend 20 minutes to turn him back into a child.

• • •

Children are the most fun you can have with your hands full.

49

Mummy

If you get divorced your children
might put you in a home
for unmarried mothers.

• • •

Remember, health visitors
were children once.

Mummy

50

Pregnancy is the speedbump on the
highway of a woman's life.

• • •

Mothers find it hard to relax
because they feel
more comfortable tense.

Mummy

A child will never come quietly –
you have to use earplugs.

• • •

They say that a child
is incapable of sin.
Yeah right!

Mummy

Children's partying
is such sweet sorrow.

• • •

Teenage haircuts
have to be believed
to be seen.

53

Mummy

With child-rearing, after all is said
and done, more is said than done.

• • •

The trouble with having a baby
is you can't get out of it. There are
no loopholes in birth certificates.

Mummy

54

Motherhood: the biggest on-the-job training programme around.

• • •

A mum's life begins when the kids leave home and ends when they bring back the laundry.

Mummy

When you have a one-year-old
he brings you hugs all the time.
When he's two he brings you bugs
all the time. By the time he's 16
he just bugs you all the time.

Mummy

56

When buying clothes, children are always keen to add to the merchandising revenue of cartoon heroes. Someone ought to make a film featuring the animated St Michael.

Mummy

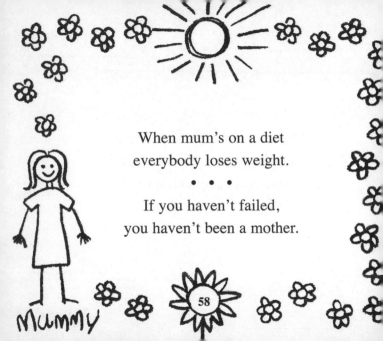

When mum's on a diet
everybody loses weight.

• • •

If you haven't failed,
you haven't been a mother.

58

Mummy

A child is a test you will always fail.

• • •

A mother is someone who sees
three pieces of cake for four people
and then announces that she's
never liked cake.

MUMMY

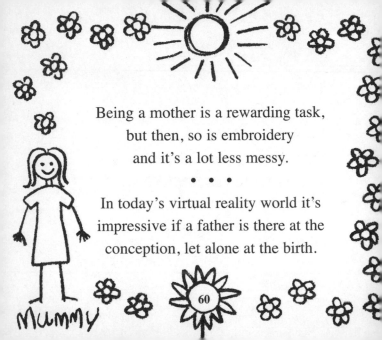

Being a mother is a rewarding task,
but then, so is embroidery
and it's a lot less messy.

• • •

In today's virtual reality world it's
impressive if a father is there at the
conception, let alone at the birth.

60

MUMMY

Working mothers need to be
accomplished jugglers.
If they lose concentration
for a moment they could easily
drop a husband or two.

61

Mummy

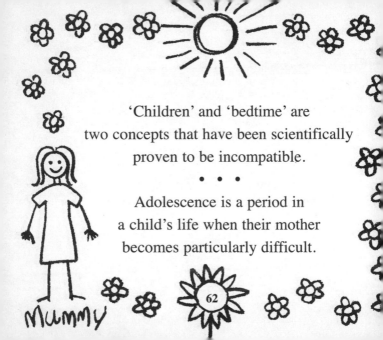

'Children' and 'bedtime' are
two concepts that have been scientifically
proven to be incompatible.

• • •

Adolescence is a period in
a child's life when their mother
becomes particularly difficult.

Mummy

With kids' clothes it's a question
of what wears out first – the clothes or
the mother's patience.

• • •

The boss of the family is the one
with the executive potty.

Mummy

In the first two years of
a child's life you try to get her
to talk. For the next ten years
you'll try everything else
to get her to stop.

Mummy

64

The moment you let your children go to make their way in the world is the moment they decide it's cheaper to move back in with you.

65

mummy

Adolescents are children who've stopped asking questions because they now know all the answers.

• • •

Television destroys the art of conversation, and crying, whining, screaming…

MUMMY

66

Every mother knows that a child goes
from wonderful to playful to hateful
without ever passing grateful.

• • •

Children can always spot a lie.
Teenagers lie about their spots.

How to tell a mother's true age –
take what she tells you and add
the age of her child.

• • •

Enjoy your time in hospital
after the birth. That's the last sleep
you'll get.

68

Mummy

If children have a sweet tooth,
why do they have a foul mouth?

• • •

Brothers always blame each other.
If that fails they blame their mother.

69

Mummy

The ideal child-carer –
you with Bill Gates's bank account.

• • •

Not only is a woman's work
never done, but no one's ever issued
her a job description.

MuMMy

70

The best time to get children to bed is while you still have the strength.

• • •

A small child's idea of helping with the housework is to lick melted chocolate off the bedroom carpet.

Mummy

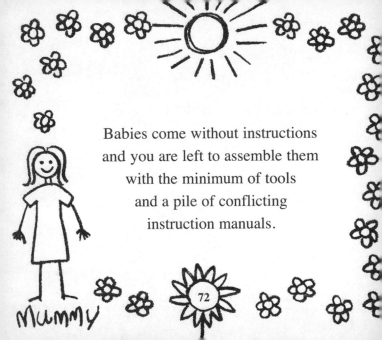

Babies come without instructions
and you are left to assemble them
with the minimum of tools
and a pile of conflicting
instruction manuals.

Mummy

72

No matter what you do
a boy will behave just like his dad –
throwing tantrums, buying
big toys and sulking if
he doesn't get his own way.

73

Mummy

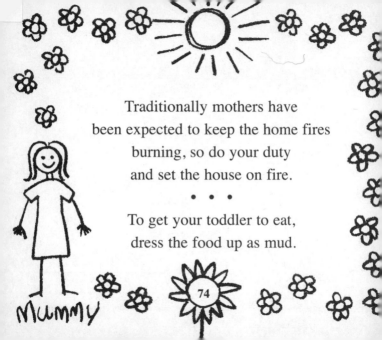

Traditionally mothers have
been expected to keep the home fires
burning, so do your duty
and set the house on fire.

• • •

To get your toddler to eat,
dress the food up as mud.

Mummy

Mothers should always have a partner around because too many things in life go wrong to blame them all on the government.

• • •

Pity the child in the harem trying to celebrate Mother's Day.

mummy

Having carpet fitted in a bathroom with small boys in the house is like having the newspaper delivered to your shower.

• • •

By the time your child is 12 months old he should be eating solids: keys, pencils, your slippers…

Mummy

There is nothing wrong with the world
that mum couldn't sort out with a few
sharp words in one afternoon.

• • •

Create some time for yourself.
Pack the children off to school then
quietly move house.

Mummy

Force-feed your children
every type of television programme
going, day and night, seven days a week.
By the time they're at nursery school
they'll be begging to swop Richard
and Judy for Janet and John.

Mummy

78

Stop your children dumping clothes all over the house. Wash them all together and claim you thought they wanted all their white shirts to be pink.

• • •

Cleanliness is to children what Princess Diana is to heavyweight boxing.

Mummy

Remember, only a
15-year-old girl knows what love is.

• • •

Show me a mother who doesn't
feel guilty and I'll show you a father.

80

Mummy

Becoming a mother means that you suddenly learn how to be shocked.

• • •

The best time to discuss sex with your children is once you're both divorced.

Mummy

Of course mothers can't have everything –
they wouldn't have anywhere to put it.

• • •

A mother should never face facts.
If she did she'd never
get up in the morning.

Mummy

82

When children ask you where they came from, don't pretend you know.

• • •

If you're a mother it's OK to let yourself go, so long as you can let yourself back in again.

Mummy

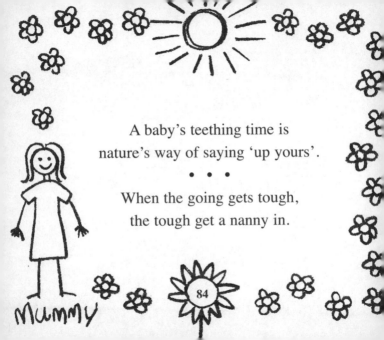

A baby's teething time is
nature's way of saying 'up yours'.

• • •

When the going gets tough,
the tough get a nanny in.

84

Children can choose their friends
but they only have one mum.

• • •

To mothers, life is what happens
in between the washing.

85

Support wildlife: throw a birthday party
for your two-year-old.

• • •

Mothers of schoolchildren are faced
with a cruel choice –
a job or daytime television.

Mummy

A teenager will never put off
till tomorrow what he can get his mum
to do for him today.

• • •

There are only two things that small
children are willing to share with
anyone: their germs and your age.

Mummy

The most useful appliance a mother
can have in the home is a partner
with a large salary.

• • •

Mothers need to give their children
so much love there's enough spare
to be flung back at them.

88

MuMMY

Why do family and friends
send presents to a new-born baby?
After all, it didn't do the work.

• • •

There is only one perfect child
in the world and
every mother has it.

Mummy

A mother's true joy is secret,
and so is her age.

• • •

Mothers are the bones on which
children sharpen their teeth.

Mummy

A child's tears: the most effective
power shower.

• • •

Child's law of strawberry jam: it should
be found on walls, doorhandles
and hair but never on bread.

Mother's Day –
so-called because mum
gets to spend an extra ten minutes
in bed and the rest of the day
being a mother.

Mummy

92

To avoid tears on the first day of school –

1) get the uniform just right
2) pack their favourite food for lunch
3) remind yourself they'll be back in the afternoon and you won't be alone for the whole day.

93

MUMMY

Take time out every now and then.
It's much less tiring than taking
the children out.

• • •

It's only natural for a mother to have
favourites, unless you only have
one child, and she's not your favourite.

Mummy

It's always the child from the germ-free home who is first to catch the measles.

• • •

Mothering is a hard job. If it were easy you'd have consultants charging £100 an hour to do it.

Mummy

At bedtime mothers have to put up with constant whining, procrastination and excuses – but then fathers are like that.

• • •

Everyone should be pro natural childbirth. After all, who wants an unnatural child?

Mummy

96

No one tells you that the saying
'there'll be tears before bedtime' actually
refers to mothers who use the time to
give themselves a bikini wax.

• • •

Mothers never cry over spilt milk –
provided its not their own.

Mummy

When your teenage son berates you for being uncool remind him that he's the one who used to stuff peas up his nose.

• • •

Motherhood is like a bowl of cherries: sometimes it's sweet and sometimes it's the pits.

Mummy

98

Sons are cheaper than daughters.
After all, you only
have to buy one earring.

• • •

When you were single you used to
rock till dawn. Now you're a new
mother, you still do.

mummy

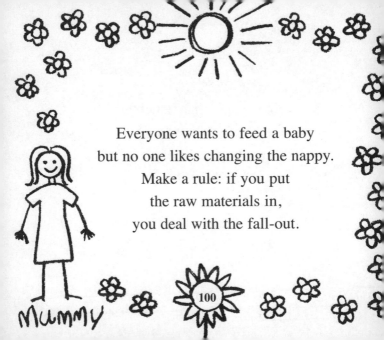

Everyone wants to feed a baby
but no one likes changing the nappy.
Make a rule: if you put
the raw materials in,
you deal with the fall-out.

Mummy

100

There are only three obstacles to calm, thoughtful child-rearing:
1) Exhaustion
2) Exhaustion
3) Exhaustion

Mummy

A radical midwife: the red next to the bed.

• • •

Everyone says that when
the baby arrives you'll lose
all the weight you gained during
the pregnancy. No one tells you it's
because you're too tired to eat.

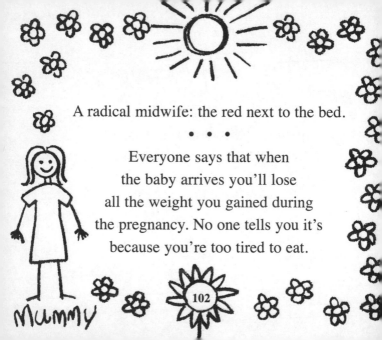

Some mothers have to have
an estate car because after they've
finished chauffeuring the children
to private nursery, fee-paying school,
ballet, tennis lessons and
private tuition, the car is all that's
left of the estate.

103

Mummy

Every woman should have children, if only
to have someone in the house who can
programme the video recorder.

• • •

When you despair of them ever becoming
potty-trained remember that very few
people leave university in nappies.

Mummy

Women without children dream
of romance, wealth and success.
Mothers dream of sleep.

• • •

Remember, child bowel movements
are not a topic of fascination to
your single friends.

105

Mummy

Out of the mouths of babes
comes the stuff you spent hours
preparing in the blender.

• • •

Buy all the books on child-rearing
you can find. They're very useful
for propping up broken furniture.

Mummy

Things you'll never hear your partner say:
1) Oh no, let me get up, it's only three in the morning
2) Don't worry, I'll tell them about sex
3) I think those puffy eyes, extra wrinkles and the milk stains on your blouse are the sexiest things ever.

Mummy

Things you'll never say to your partner:
1) (During birth) I'm so glad you made me pregnant
2) (After the birth) I feel so sorry for the agony you went through while I had the baby

Mummy

108

3) Of course you can spend the weekend watching football with your mates. Entertaining the kids on my own is what I live for.

• • •

Don't try to be cool.
Mothering is a hot job.

Mummy

The only guarantee of knowing
how to deal properly with your child
is not to be its mother.

• • •

A little vagueness
goes a long way.

Children don't like moral stories –
they like the ones where innocent
people get crushed to death and
the small ugly boy becomes king.

• • •

When in doubt, shout.

When you are pregnant you have to
eat for two, but remember the other one is
the size of a newt, not Marlon Brando.

• • •

If you want to tell your children
something important, say it softly
to someone else.

112

Mummy

Don't be too ambitious for your children.
If they grow up able to refrain from using
words such as 'hospitalisation' and
'diarise' you've been a successful mother.

• • •

If you can't keep up with your
children drag them down to your level.

113

Mummy

Never pass comment on your
teenage daughter's clothes –
it'll only encourage her.

• • •

Don't try to make your children
like you. Mothers should be
loved not liked.

114

Mummy

Have as many children as possible.
That way you'll always be able to put
someone in the fast-moving queue.

• • •

If you're the kind of mother
that irons underpants
you don't deserve to rest.

115

Mummy

If something's worth doing, it's worth getting your children to do it for you.

• • •

Don't serve skimmed milk to growing children. Pouring non-fat milk on your cereal is like talking to yourself.

Mummy

If a baby smiles at you it's because:

    a) He loves you

    b) He's got wind

    c) He's just learnt to smile

    d) He's just thought of a joke

    e) You are the joke.

Mummy

Having a baby changes everything –
in particular what you are wearing
while it's feeding.

• • •

Maternity clothes –
like maternity wards but bigger and
with less sense of style.

Mummy

If you have an important message you
want your children to remember and
repeat clearly make sure you include in it
at least one swear word.

• • •

What is a home without children?
Tidy.

119

Mummy

If you think you've missed out on life by having children, sit in a career-woman's office for a day and check out the childish behaviour she has to deal with every day.

• • •

If you have more than four children you're overbearing.

Mummy

120

The majority of babies are lulled to sleep by the sound of vacuuming. So give them a hand – the moment they're out of the womb, get them doing the housework.

• • •

Telling people you are 'just a mother' is like calling the Queen 'just a monarch'.

Mummy

Mother's Pride is well-bread children.

• • •

If you have a child-carer who dotes on
your child, will come at a moment's
notice and doesn't mind how long they
stay – you've got a granny.

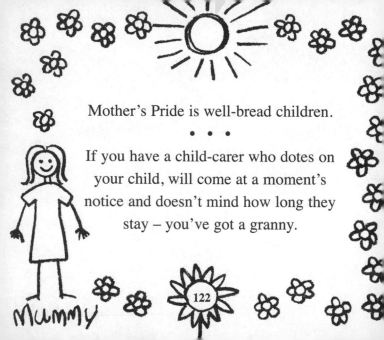

If you're the sort of mother who doesn't mind how much mess your children make, doesn't worry about entertaining them and loves to hear them creating mayhem in the garden – you're a mother with a nanny.

123

You're not a true mother unless you have done a complete course in martyrdom.

• • •

Throwing a birthday party for a small child is like childbirth itself. After both events you promise yourself you'll never ever be stupid enough to do it again.

Mummy

If you always try to see
the children's point of view,
half kill yourself helping with
homework and do all
you can to make them like you,
you're a step-mother.

Mummy

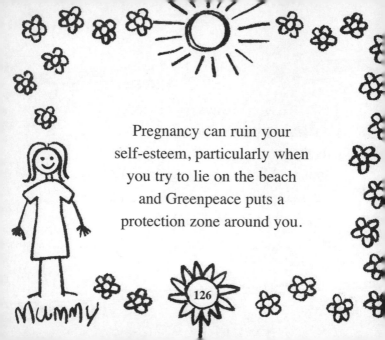

Pregnancy can ruin your
self-esteem, particularly when
you try to lie on the beach
and Greenpeace puts a
protection zone around you.

Mummy

The best thing about giving birth
is the size of your breasts. For most
of us its the only time we'll ever
get an idea of what it must be like
to be Pamela Anderson.

Jasmine Birtles has an international reputation, but we won't hold that against her. She has written widely on childcare in over fourteen languages, many of them at the same time, and still manages to collect the children from the eighteen-year-old Czech girl she leaves them with most of the week. Her first book, widely hailed as the most important event in publishing since Edison discovered support tights, was entitled 'The Leg-Waxer's Reading List'. Her services to motherhood were finally recognised in 1992 when she was decorated by the Duchess of Kent with a set of stencils and some poster paints. She died a year later and went on to work for the Child Support Agency.

Mummy